Ludwig van Beethoven
(1770 - 1827)

Sonaten

für Klavier · for piano · pour piano

I

Urtext

Herausgegeben von · Edited by · Edité par
István Máriássy & Tamás Zászkaliczky
K 107
Könemann Music Budapest

INDEX

I

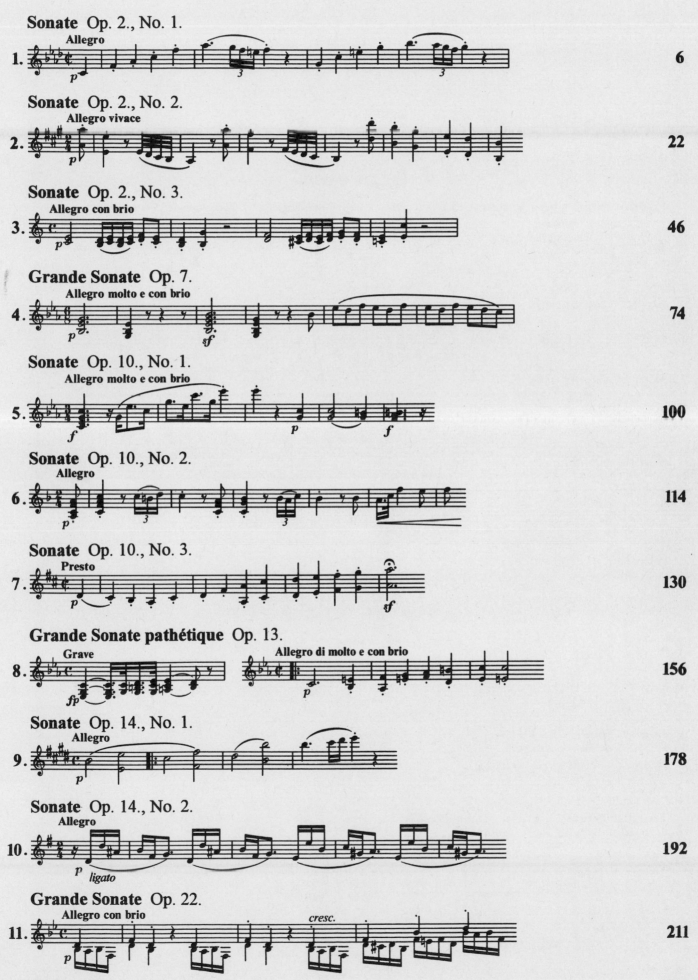

INDEX

II

 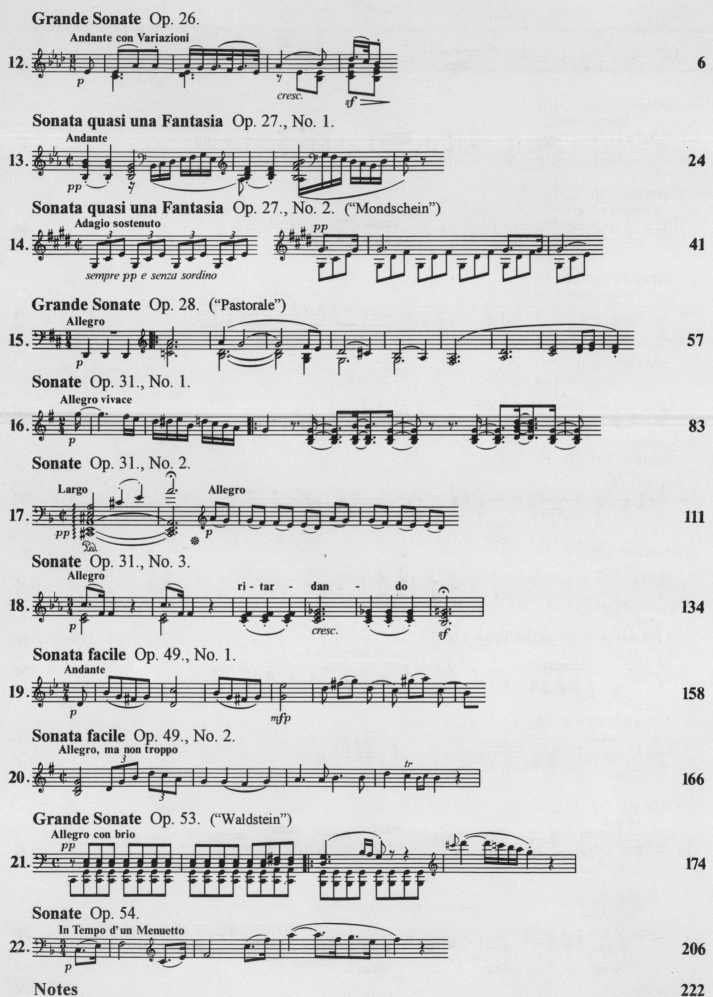

INDEX

III

Sonate

pour le clavecin ou pianoforte

Op. 2., No. 1.
1795

Adagio

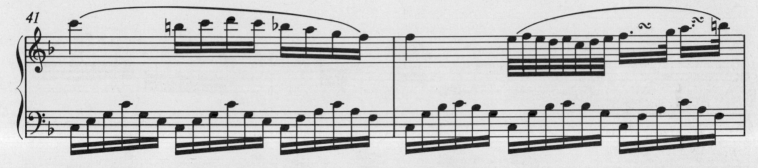

K 107

Menuetto
Allegretto

14

Prestissimo

sempre piano e dolce

K 107

21

Joseph Haydn gewidmet

Sonate

pour le clavecin ou pianoforte

Op. 2., No. 2.
1795

Allegro vivace

2.

22

K 107

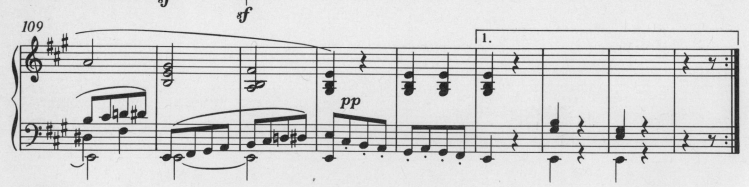

24

28

Largo appassionato

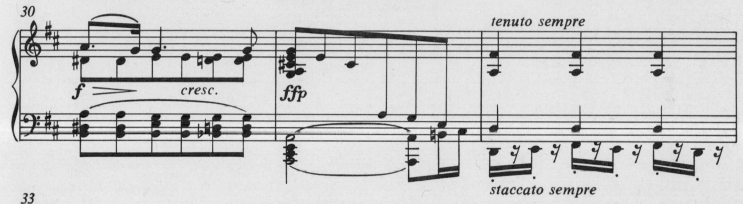

tenuto sempre

staccato sempre

Scherzo
Allegretto

Minore

Scherzo D. C.

Rondo
Grazioso

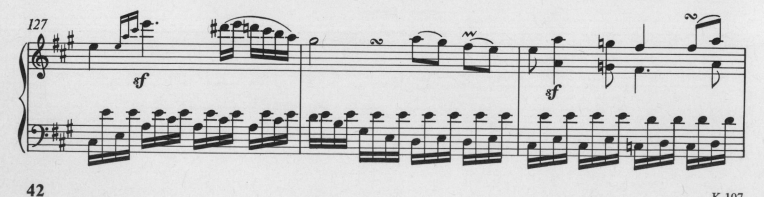

42

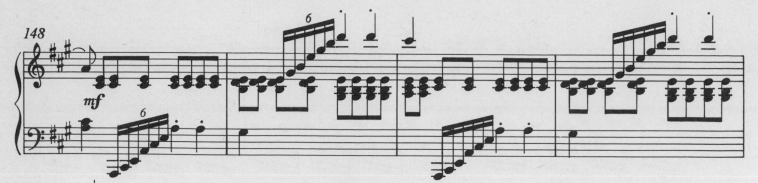

Sonate

pour le clavecin ou pianoforte

Op. 2., No. 3.
1795

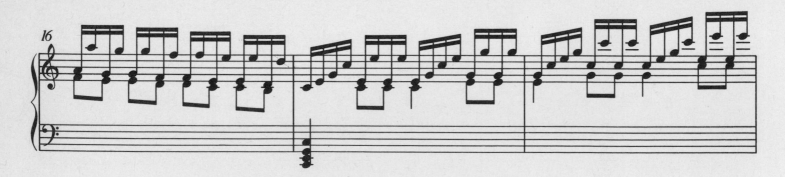

50

K 107

58

Trio

Scherzo D.C.
e poi la Coda

Allegro assai

Grande Sonate

pour le clavecin ou pianoforte

Op. 7.
1796–97

Allegro molto e con brio

4.

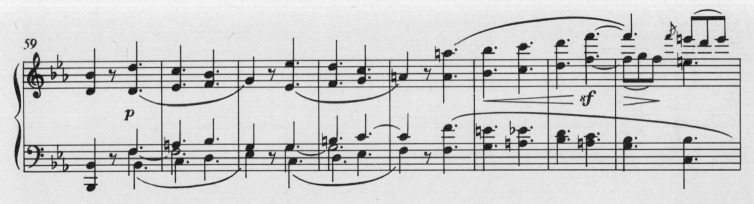

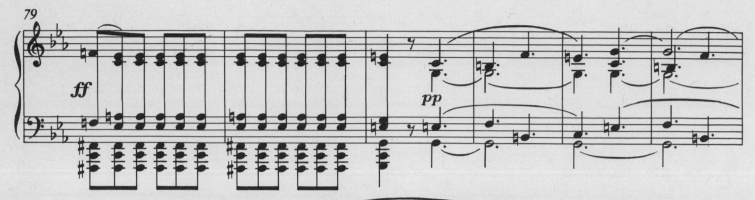

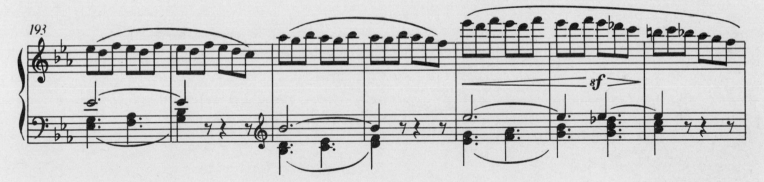

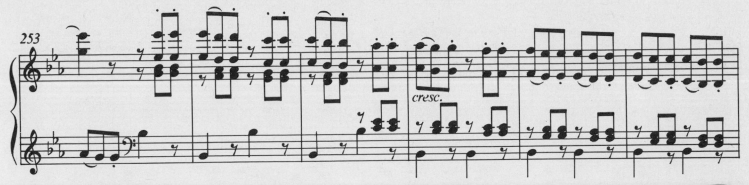

Largo, con gran espressione

sempre stacc.

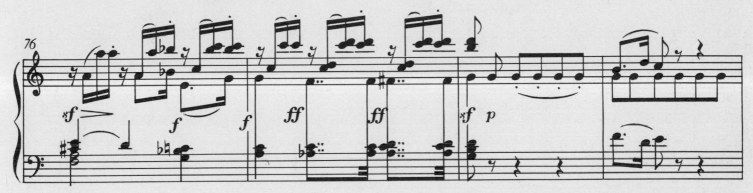

Allegro

Minore

Rondo
Poco Allegretto e grazioso

92

ri - tar - dan - do pp

K 107

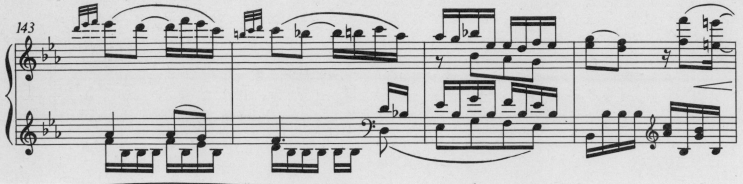

Sonate

pour le clavecin ou pianoforte

Op. 10., No. 1.
1796–98

Allegro molto e con brio

K 107

104

K 107

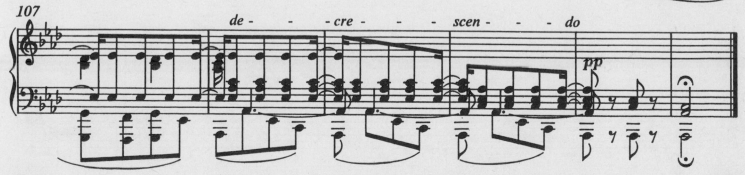

Finale
Prestissimo

112

Sonate

pour le clavecin ou pianoforte

Op. 10., No. 2.
1796–98

Allegro

6.

K 107

115

120

122

Presto

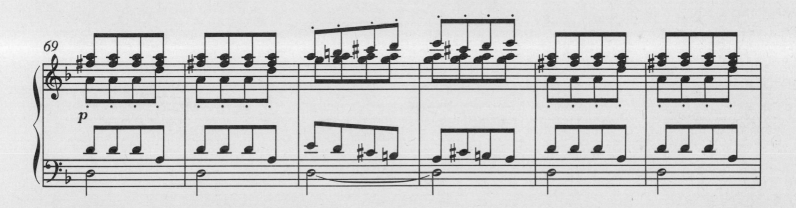

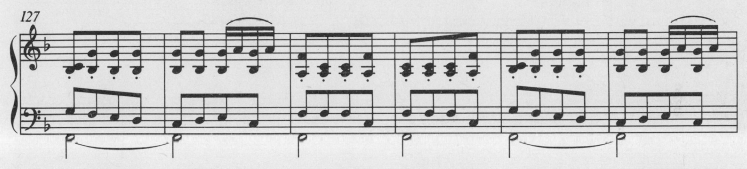

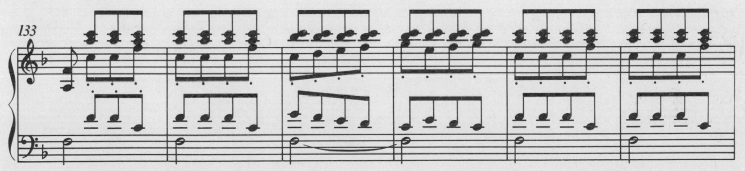

Sonate
pour le clavecin ou pianoforte

Op. 10., No. 3.
1796–98

7.

136

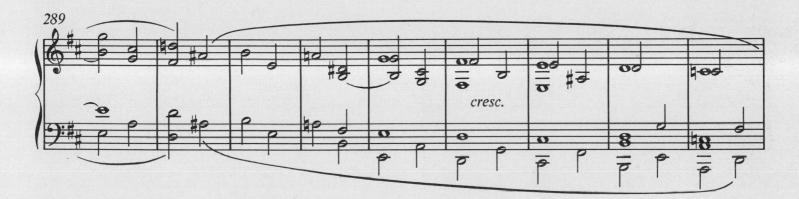

Largo e mesto

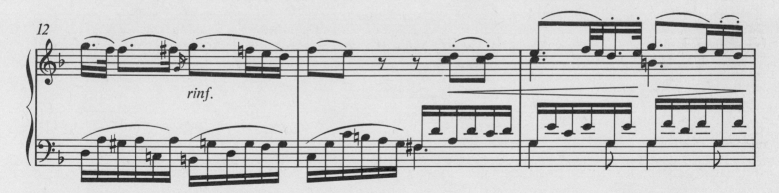

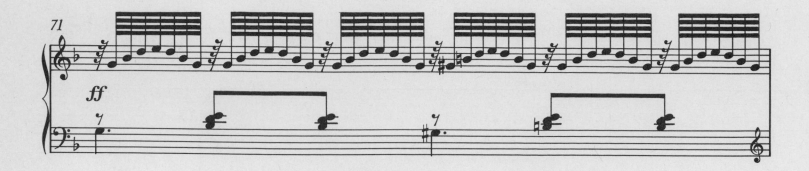

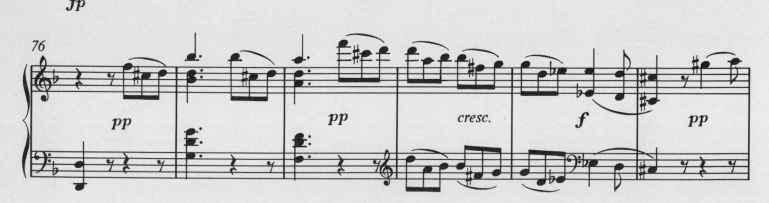

146

Menuetto
Allegro

Men. D.C., ma senza replica

Rondo
Allegro

150

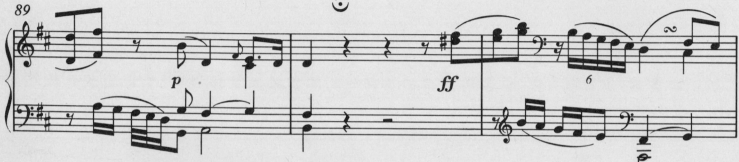

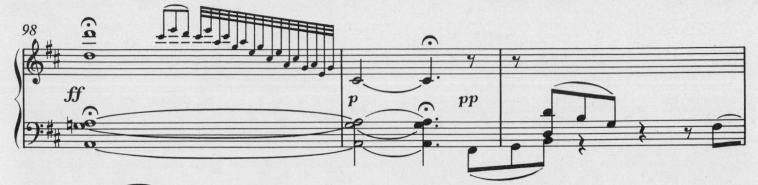

Grande Sonate pathétique

pour le clavecin ou pianoforte

Op. 13.
1798–99

Grave

8.

attacca subito il Allegro:

K 107

Allegro di molto e con brio

K 107

attacca subito Allegro
molto e con brio

a) Sustain the hold (pause) three full bars (comp. $\begin{Bmatrix}\text{Note a,}\\ \text{(Page 112);}\end{Bmatrix}$ the first holds in the *Grave* have precisely the same duration (subtracting the demisemiquaver).

b) The bass note on the third crotchet must have a penetrating and prolonged tone, in order to be quite audible through the seventh quaver as the root of the chord of the sixth.

c) This coda cannot be played too rapidly.

d) It is best not to use the pedal with these chords.

11611

Adagio cantabile

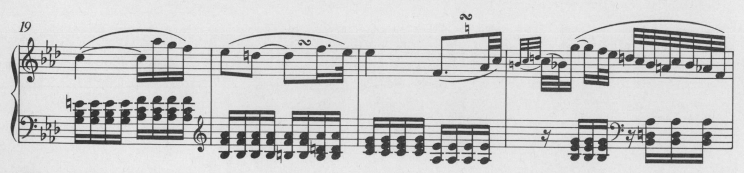

K 107

Rondo
Allegro

174

ca - - lan -

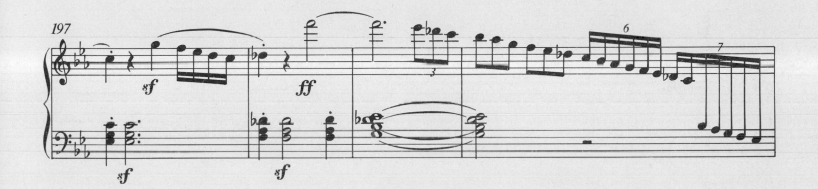

Sonate
pour le pianoforte

Op. 14., No. 1.
1798–99

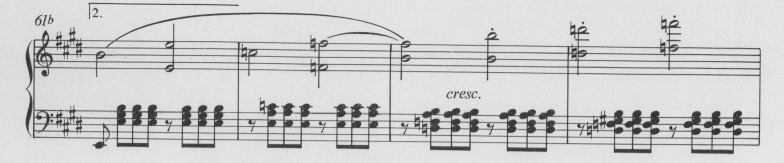

182

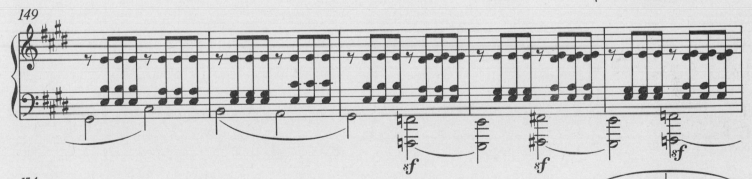

K 107

Allegretto

Rondo

Allegro comodo

K 107

189

Sonate

pour le pianoforte

Op. 14., No. 2.
1798–99

Allegro

10.

192

K 107

K 107

194

196

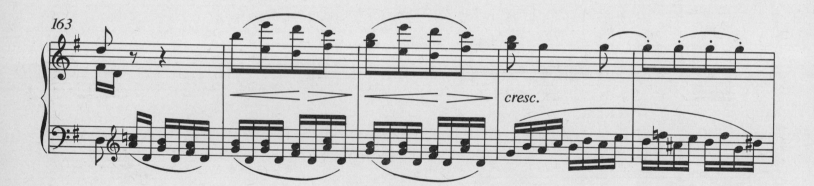

Andante
La prima parte senza replica

202

Scherzo

Allegro assai

K 107

Grande Sonate

pour le pianoforte

Op. 22.
1799–1800

212

K 107

216

Adagio con molta espressione

224

Minore

Minuetto D.C. senza replica

Rondo

Allegretto

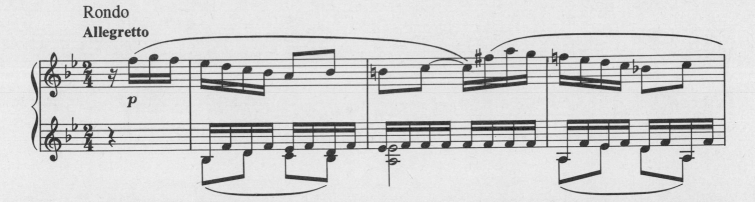

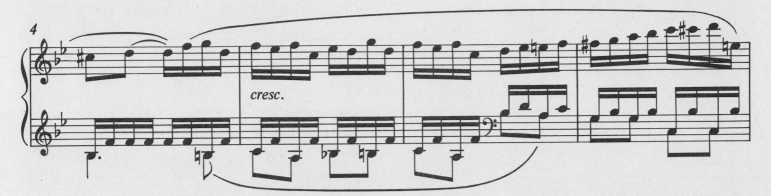

K 107

K 107

232

K 107

234

Notes

The present edition is based on the autograph manuscript and/or first edition(s) of the works. Other early editions have also been consulted, whenever justified.

The editorial additions reduced to a minimum appear in square brackets. The additions are restricted to notes and signs missing in the sources, deemed nevertheless absolutely necessary. The evident slips of the pen and printing errors have been tacitly corrected. Similarly, signs omitted due to the perfunctory manner of notation (staccato marks, slurs, dynamics, etc.) are added without comment. The octave passages have been supplemented by adding lower and upper notes which Beethoven did not write due to the limited pitch of the contemporary keyboard. Staccato is indicated by a dot throughout.

No additions by analogy have been made. This explains why the expression marks not available in the sources but included in most modern editions are missing in this edition. In regard to the manner of performance, the execution of ornaments and fingering no suggestions have been made.

The title and dedication of the works as well as the specification of the instruments are given according to the sources.

The considerable inconsistencies of the sources are listed below.

1: Sonata in F Minor op. 2/1
1st movt., bar 140, lower staff, beat 4, the chord in the source:

4th movt., bars 131-132: the tie of the bass is missing in the source.

2. Sonata in A Major op. 2/2
1st movt., bar 104, upper staff: in some modern editions there is an e^1 of minim value here by analogy with bar 324.
1st movt., bar 203, the upper staff appears in the source as:

3. Sonata in C Major op. 2/3
1st movt., bars 223, 225, 227: the first notes of the chords in the upper staff were emended in semibreve by Beethoven subsequently. The first edition has minims.
4th movt., bar 210, upper staff: some modern editions suggest *d sharp³* for the upper note of the chord.

4. Sonata in E♭ Major op. 7
1st movt., bar 157, in the first edition the first chord of the upper staff is:

5. Sonata in C Minor op. 10/1

1st movt., bar 36, upper staff: in the source the note *a flat*[1] of the middle part is missing.

1st movt., bar 161, upper staff: the last chord in the source is:

6. Sonata in F Major op. 10/2

1st movt., bar 5, upper staff, the rhythm of the first two notes in the source is:

2nd movt., bar 103, the second chord of the upper staff in the first edition is:

7. Sonata in D Major op. 10/3

1st movt., bar 17 appears in some modern editions as:

8. Sonata in C Minor op. 13

1st movt., bar 83, the lower staff in the source is:

9. Sonata in E Major op. 14/1

3rd movt., bar 81, the lower staff is given in some modern editions as:

11. Sonata in B♭ Major op. 22

1st movt., bar 43, the last chord of the lower staff in the sources is given as:

1st movt., bar 101: *p* comes already here in the sources.

© 1994 for this edition by Könemann Music Budapest Kft.
H-1137 Budapest, Szent István park 3.

K 107/2

Distributed worldwide by
Könemann Verlagsgesellschaft mbH · Bonner Str. 126.
D–50968 Köln

Responsible co-editor: Tamás Zászkaliczky
Production: Detlev Schaper
Technical editor: Dezső Varga
Cover design: Peter Feierabend
Engraved by Kottamester Bt., Budapest:
Edina Lakatos, Mrs. Zsuzsanna Gedai, Eszter Csontos,
Mrs. Judit Velősy, Zsuzsanna Czúni, Mrs. Zsuzsanna Mák,
Sarolta Asztalos, Mrs. Erzsébet Malaczkó

Printed by: Kner Printing House Gyomaendrőd
☎ (36) 66/386-172
Printed in Hungary

ISBN 963 8303 20 4